DAVID

Embracing the Truth

Becoming a believer

STANDARD PUBLISHING
Cincinnati, Ohio

ISBN 0-7847-1162-3

Cover design by DesignTeam

Printed in the United States of America.

Solid Foundation™ is a trademark of Standard Publishing, Cincinnati, Ohio.
A division of Standex International Corporation.

07 06 05 04 03 02 01 00
5 4 3 2 1

CONTENTS

A NOTE TO THE READER

What would it be like if God himself came to earth?

What if he were reared by a small-town, blue-collar family? What if he didn't reveal himself just to the religious leaders, but put himself into daily contact with ordinary men and women—with no-nonsense farmers and shrewd merchants? What if he rubbed elbows with soldiers and fishermen, noisy little kids and streetwise sinners?

What if he lived through the same growth phases you and I experience? The tears of infancy, the awkwardness of adolescence, the responsibilities of adulthood? What if he spoke profound words of wisdom, and careful authors wrote them down? What if he performed powerful miracles, and eyewitnesses recorded them in a book for all mankind to read?

Instead of having an easy time of it here on earth, what if God faced intense suffering—physical anguish, emotional rejection, social injustice, spiritual agony? What if he died—a violent, painful, humiliating death? And then, what if he came back to life again?

According to the Bible, that's exactly what happened. About 2,000 years ago, God did come to earth. An ancient prophet referred to him as "Immanuel," which means "God with us." He was born to a virgin named Mary in the Middle-Eastern village of Bethlehem and reared by a carpenter named Joseph in the obscure village of Nazareth. Beginning at age 30, he gathered around himself a group of disciples who heard him teach, witnessed his miracles, and gradually came to recognize him as the Son of God.

Some of his followers wrote about him. One, a fisherman named John, called Jesus "the Word" who "became flesh and lived for a while among us." Jesus "came to that which was his own," John pointed out, "but his own did not receive him." Some did receive him, however. And "to all who received him, to those who believed in his name, he gave the right to become children of God" (John 1:11, 12).

Up-Close With God

Later John described Jesus in greater detail: "That which was from the beginning, which we have heard, which we have seen with our eyes, which we have looked at and our hands have touched—this we proclaim concerning the Word of life. The life appeared; we have seen it and testify to it, and we proclaim to you the eternal life, which was with the Father and has appeared to us" (1 John 1:1, 2).

What would it be like to know the Lord so closely, so personally?

In the country church I attended as a boy, two large paintings hung on the front wall, one at either side of the pulpit. One showed Jesus holding little children in his arms. The other showed a shepherd carrying a lamb in his arms.

I loved those paintings—even though as a young boy I didn't understand them.

Later I read in the Bible how Jesus invited the little children to come to him, and he took them in his arms and blessed them (Mark 10:16). I read that the Lord "tends his flock like a shepherd: He gathers the lambs in his arms and carries them close to his heart" (Isaiah 40:11).

Does God really care that much about people who have lost their way? So much that he wants to embrace us—to hold us in his arms?

Love That Reaches Out

To illustrate the love of God, Jesus told about a shepherd who valued each sheep in his flock. Even though he has 99 sheep safe in the pen, the shepherd searches diligently for the one sheep that's still missing. When the shepherd finds the lost sheep, "he joyfully puts it on his shoulders" and takes it home (Luke 15:1-7). Some see God as aloof, distant, and unapproachable—keeping people at arm's length. But according to Jesus, he's like a shepherd who finds the runaway sheep and then gives it a joyful piggyback ride on the way back to the barn!

In another story, Jesus told about a young man who squandered his life in wild living. Finally, in a time of desperate need, the young man returned home, humble and remorseful. "But while he was still a long way off," Jesus said, "his father saw him and was filled with compassion for him; he ran to his son, threw his arms around him and kissed him" (Luke 15:20).

That's how Jesus painted a picture of the love of God. It's a love that reaches out. A love that holds us firmly in the strong arms of our heavenly Father.

A love that embraces.

Not at Arm's Length

In the pages that follow, you can read the true stories of some men and women who decided to return God's embrace. If you're thinking about becoming a Christian, their stories can help you take another step in your spiritual journey.

To get the most out of this little book, you need two things: a Bible and a Christian friend. By reading the Scripture references provided, you will get better acquainted with God's Word and his will for your life. By discussing this material with a

Christian friend, you can find answers to your own unique questions and concerns.

God has reached out to us in love. Don't keep him at arm's length. Open your heart to him and reach back.

Embrace the truth.

Cincinnati, Ohio

A THIRSTY OUTCAST: HEARING THE SOUND OF HOPE

She was surprised he spoke to her at all.

Not that it was uncommon for men to notice her. She'd already been married five times, and now she was living with a man who wasn't her husband. But for a man to talk with her–and really listen to her–well, that was another story.

Like other women in her village, she came to draw water from the public well. Unlike most of them, though, she didn't come in the cool of the morning but at midday. Better to endure the hot sun than the withering gaze of the town gossips.

Carrying her empty water jar, the woman could see a stranger sitting by the well. A Jewish man? What was he doing here? Typically, Jewish people avoided traveling through her homeland of Samaria altogether. Jews and Samaritans didn't mix. They were like cats and dogs, oil and water–like corresponding poles on a magnet. But there he was, looking weary, perhaps from a long journey on foot.

"Will you give me a drink?" he asked.

Startled, the woman nearly dropped her water jar.

"You are a Jew and I am a Samaritan woman," she said, stating the obvious. "How can you ask me for a drink?"

"If you knew the gift of God and who it is that asks you for a drink, you would have asked him and he would have given you living water," the stranger said.

The gift of God? Living water? What was this stranger talking about? Normally she might have walked away. But this time the woman couldn't ignore her own curiosity. There was a purity about the stranger's gaze. An unvarnished sincerity about his words.

She decided to continue the conversation. "Sir, you have nothing to draw with and the well is deep. Where can you get this living water?"

The well had been there outside her village for centuries. "Are you greater than our father Jacob," she went on, "who gave us this well and drank from it himself, as did also his sons and his flocks and herds?"

"Everyone who drinks this water will be thirsty again," replied the stranger. "But whoever drinks the water I give him will never thirst."

If You Knew the Gift of God

The stranger in this story was Jesus. The woman? An unnamed resident of Sychar, a Samaritan village located about 25 miles north of Jerusalem. The complete story appears in the fourth chapter of the Gospel of John, a book filled with fascinating truth about the Son of God.

It's John who tells us that "the Word" (that is, Jesus Christ) "became flesh and lived for a while among us" (1:14). He's the one who writes about Jesus' first miracle, changing water into wine (2:1-11). He records Jesus' conversation with Nicodemus, where Jesus says it's necessary to be born again to enter the kingdom of God (3:1-8). John also writes one of the most famous Bible verses of all, John 3:16, which says, "For God so loved the world that he gave his one and only Son, that whoever believes in him shall not perish but have eternal life."

In a way, the rest of John's Gospel simply illustrates that one key verse. It's a book about God's love—

his flawless, deep, abiding love–a love that embraces us even when we're at life's lowest ebb. God loves people like Nicodemus, a respected religious leader well-schooled in the Bible but still in need of a closer walk with God. And God loves people like the Samaritan woman, who received respect from almost no one but found a friend in Jesus when he sat down by the well and talked to her about eternal life.

That day by the well, the woman didn't realize it at first, but she was face to face with God's love in personal form. Jesus brought her a gift she desperately needed but was only beginning to understand. In one of the longest personal conversations of Jesus recorded anywhere in Scripture, she heard the truth of God from the lips of the Lord, and became his committed follower even though there's no indication that she ever saw him perform a miracle.

It was enough that she simply heard his words.

The Words and Ways of Jesus

By bringing God's good news to this Samaritan woman, Jesus ignored the prejudice that caused Jews and Samaritans to avoid each other. He ignored the social customs of his day that said a man shouldn't address a woman in public. He ignored his own weariness and thirst, putting her spiritual needs above his own need for rest and refreshment.

Even though he'd never met her before, Jesus knew she had been married five times, and that she was living with a man who was not her husband.

"Sir, I can see that you are a prophet," she admitted. Then, perhaps uncomfortable with the personal direction this conversation was taking, she brought up another topic. The Samaritans worship God "on this mountain," she pointed out, "but you Jews claim that the place where we must worship is in Jerusalem."

If she meant to create a conversational detour, Jesus steered deftly around it. "Salvation is from the Jews," he said, for God worked through the Jewish people to bring the Scriptures and the good news of salvation to all mankind. But the deeper truth about worship, Jesus insisted, is that "God is spirit, and his worshipers must worship in spirit and in truth."

"I know that Messiah" (a word for Christ, God's

anointed king and deliverer) "is coming," the woman said. "When he comes, he will explain everything to us."

And Jesus told her, "I who speak to you am he."

Have You Heard the Sound of Hope?

The Bible says, "Faith comes from hearing the message, and the message is heard through the word of Christ" (Romans 10:17).

You and I haven't heard the actual voice of God thundering from the sky. But his message rings true from the pages of Scripture. When we read the claims of Jesus recorded in John's Gospel and the rest of God's Word, we're hearing the truth–truth that can fuel our hope, build our faith, and give us spiritual freedom (John 8:32).

Jesus doesn't sit down and talk with us in the middle of the day by a well. Yet, in a sense, Christ comes to all of us much the way he came to the Samaritan woman. He goes where you wouldn't expect him to go–a perfect Savior walking among imperfect, sinful people–to bring a gift we could not earn or deserve. He does it because God doesn't want any of us to die in our sins, eternally separated from him. He "is patient . . . not wanting anyone to perish, but everyone to come to repentance" (2 Peter 3:9).

In the Old Testament, God said, "My people have committed two sins: They have forsaken me, the spring of living water, and have dug their own cisterns, broken cisterns that cannot hold water" (Jeremiah 2:13). Have you been trying to drink out of a broken cistern? Do your religious beliefs really hold water? Is it time you listened to the honest, life-giving words of Jesus? He offers a spring of living water that will never run dry.

And oh, by the way: The Scriptures never tell us whether or not the woman at the well actually gave Jesus a drink of water. Evidently, in his opinion, the more important thirst to be quenched that day was hers.

REFLECTIONS

For discussion with a Christian friend:

1. What do you think the Bible means when it talks about how "faith comes from hearing" (Romans 10:17)?

2. What did Jesus mean when he promised to give the woman at the well "living water"?

3. Jeremiah 2:13 talks about "broken cisterns"—religious beliefs and practices that don't hold water. Can any amount of money, work, entertainment, sexual pleasure, popularity, or even religious devotion satisfy a soul's thirst for God? Has your life ever contained any "broken cisterns" that have left you unsatisfied?

For further reading:

- About the seriousness of sin: Romans 3:23; Colossians 1:21; James 2:10; 1 John 1:8-10
- About God's love for all people: Acts 10:34-36; Galatians 3:26-29; 1 John 2:1, 2
- About God's gift of eternal life: Romans 6:23; Ephesians 2:1-10; Titus 3:3-7
- About God's willingness to quench our spiritual thirst: John 7:37-39; Revelation 22:17

A DESPISED TAXMAN: SEEING THROUGH THE EYES OF FAITH

The last thing anyone expected Jesus to do was call a man like Matthew to be his disciple. Matthew was a publican–someone who collected public funds. He lived in Capernaum, a bustling first-century trade center located on the edge of the Sea of Galilee. Caravans passed through on their way north from Egypt or west toward the Mediterranean. Near the boat docks, sailors sold their daily catches of fish. A lot of money changed hands in Capernaum, and a lot of it ended up in Matthew's hands.

Tax collectors have never been popular, but they were especially despised in Jesus' day. Most people viewed tax collectors with about the same mistrust you and I would feel toward a drug dealer and a crooked politician rolled into one.

There were no tax forms to fill out in those days, so most people didn't know how much they were supposed to pay. Tax collectors swindled the poor and took bribes from the rich. Their Jewish neighbors considered them traitors, for they took money from the

Jews and sent it off to the Roman authorities who ruled Israel at the time. Even the coins the tax collectors handled were offensive to the Jewish faith, for they were stamped with pagan inscriptions and images.

Archaeologists have found the remains of a large Jewish synagogue in Capernaum, but Matthew probably wasn't welcome there in the house of worship. If he did attend, it's likely he sat alone.

But when Jesus saw him sitting at his tax collector's booth, he told Matthew, "Follow me."

Notice, Jesus didn't say, "Understand everything about me." He didn't say, "Analyze me," or even "Feel excited about me." He said, "Follow me."

Nor did he tell Matthew, "Follow this set of rules," "Follow what your friends are doing," or even "Follow your own emotions." Jesus said, "Follow me."

And Matthew did–exchanging his corrupt past as a tax collector for the life-changing adventure of following Christ. Fortunately, when Matthew left his tax collector's booth, he took along his pen! He wrote 28 chapters of eye-witness truth about Jesus, and the first book of the New Testament bears his name.

Sheep Who Need A Shepherd

The Lord almost seems to take delight in doing the unexpected–even calling unlikely people to be his disciples. A young businesswoman had no interest in being a Christian, but when her boss's wife invited her to a home Bible study, she found herself strangely drawn to the love of God she heard her new friends discussing. She became a strong Christian, and now she uses her business expertise to help churches grow. I remember a young man who told me, "I'm not sure I even believe in God," but eventually he became a strong believer who helps teenagers find answers to their questions about God.

Jesus sees through all our pretenses and sees our true potential. The man at work who, every Monday morning, brags about his wild weekend? Jesus sees through the fake bravado and knows that deep down in his heart, the fellow realizes how empty those weekends leave him feeling. The kid at school who's always getting into trouble? The girl who suffers from intense loneliness and quiet despair? The Lord knows when we have lost our way, lost our hope, lost our direction.

Even when we appear to have it all together, there are moments when we realize we are actually "harassed and helpless, like sheep without a shepherd" (Matthew 9:36).

Taking the Step of Faith

Jesus seeks out people like Matthew–people who know they need something and someone to believe in. In fact, that's one of the themes of Matthew's book: believing in Jesus. Several instances of faith in action appear, for example, in Matthew 9:

- Friends brought their paralyzed friend to Jesus, believing that the Lord could help. Seeing their faith, Jesus forgave the man's sins and healed the man's legs (vv. 1-8).
- Matthew himself responded to Jesus' call by leaving his tax collector's booth and following the Lord–quite an act of faith (vv. 9-13).
- A woman who had been sick for 12 years was instantly healed when she simply touched the edge of Jesus' cloak. Jesus told her, "Take heart, daughter, your faith has healed you" (vv. 20-22).

• When two blind men came to Jesus, the Lord restored their sight and told them this miracle occurred "according to their faith" (vv. 27-31).

Faith is a personal choice. It's "being sure of what we hope for and certain of what we do not see" (Hebrews 11:1). "Without faith it is impossible to please God," but the good news is, God "rewards those who earnestly seek him" (Hebrews 11:6). Faith in God is what moved biblical heroes like Abraham, Moses, David, Esther, and Paul to change their world for the better. Faith, Jesus said, can even move mountains (Matthew 21:21).

Godly parents and Christian friends can teach you about faith, but at some point you must decide what you personally believe. Do you accept the fact that God exists and Jesus is truly God's Son (Hebrews 11:6; John 20:30, 31)? Have you embraced the profound truth that Jesus died on the cross and rose from the dead to rescue you from sin and death (John 3:16; Romans 5:8-10)? Do you trust Jesus enough to follow him even when you can't see where he's leading?

That's what Matthew did.

So did Marvin Whiteman. Blind since birth, Marvin is a dedicated Christian and a skilled musician. He plays the piano and sings for churches across America, and writes and records songs about his faith in Christ. As part of his work, he often performs at youth camps. At one such camp, he allowed the campers to lead him to the edge of the swimming pool, and they watched while he dove in. It's quite an act of faith for a blind man to dive into a swimming pool! But while he exercises appropriate caution–he uses a cane, and makes sure he has reliable people leading him along–Marvin also has learned there's a time to trust, and a time to dive in.

Maybe it's time for you to dive in too.

REFLECTIONS

For discussion with a Christian friend:

1. When have you taken a step of faith?

2. At this point in your spiritual journey, what do you believe about God? About life after death? About Heaven and Hell?

3. What do you believe about Jesus?

4. Are you ready to "dive in" to a deeper walk with God?

5. After Matthew became a follower of Christ, he invited several of his friends over for dinner and had Jesus join them (Matthew 9:10). Do you have friends you'd like to introduce to Jesus too? How could you reach out to them?

For further reading:

John 1:10-18
Galatians 2:20; 3:26-29
Ephesians 2:8-10
Hebrews 11:1-3, 6
1 John 5:1-5

In addition to Matthew, the Bible tells about

another tax collector whose life was dramatically changed after he met Jesus. You can read about Zacchaeus' life-changing encounter with Jesus in Luke 19:1-10.

AN UNINVITED GUEST: BREATHING THE AROMA OF GOD'S LOVE

The Pharisees were a strict group of Jewish leaders known for their meticulous concern for religious tradition. Pharisees meant "separated ones," and they tried to separate themselves from contact with anyone they considered unacceptable or unworthy. Usually in the Bible, the Pharisees seem self-righteous and power hungry. They resented Jesus and resisted his message.

But even some of them were curious about the Lord and his message. A Pharisee named Nicodemus came to Jesus for a late-night discussion about what it means to be "born again" (John 3:1-16). Another prominent leader, Joseph of Arimathea, asked permission to bury the Lord in his own family tomb (Matthew 27:57-60; John 19:38-42).

Guess Who's Coming to Dinner

Yet another Pharisee, a man named Simon, invited Jesus to his home for dinner. Some think Simon did this so he could interrogate Jesus and try to trap him in his words. Others give Simon the benefit of the doubt and assume he was open-minded, genuinely interested in knowing more about Jesus. Whatever his motivation, he must have been chagrined when a woman known all over town for her sinfulness learned that Jesus was eating at the Pharisee's house—and showed up at the dinner party.

In first-century Israel, a rich person's house often served as a social center. When an important guest came to visit, the townspeople often showed up uninvited. They might not be allowed to eat the food provided by the host, but they could sit or stand around the courtyard and listen to the conversation. Even without Simon's invitation, this sinful woman came, curious to know more about Jesus.

In those days, the Jews followed the Roman custom of reclining on low benches while they ate at the dinner table. Boldly the woman found a place right behind the bench where Jesus was reclining, near his feet. As she stood behind him, she began to weep and "wet his feet with her tears" (Luke 7:38). The Bible doesn't say why she cried. Was it because of the depth of her pain? Evidently she had been through a lot in her lifetime, and it must have touched her deeply to be around someone like Jesus who really cared. Maybe they were tears of remorse. She had sinned a lot, and being around someone like Jesus made her even more aware of her own imperfection. Or maybe they were tears of joy as she listened to Jesus talk about God's grace, mercy, and love even for people like her.

Whatever the reason, the woman burst into tears—and not just a few small tears welling up in her eyes. She wept. Sobbed. Her tears poured down like rain on Jesus' feet in what was rapidly becoming a very awkward social situation. She began to wipe Jesus' feet with the only towel available—her own long hair, poured the expensive perfume she had bought on his feet, and kissed his feet as well. While the sweet aroma of the perfume filled the air, her honest emotion and sincere repentance brought a touch of beauty to an otherwise awkward moment.

What Kind of Savior Is Jesus?

By now, Simon was becoming quite irritated. He'd planned a nice meal, and here was this woman making a scene by weeping, wiping, and wailing! The Pharisees believed the very touch of an immoral woman made you unclean. Plus, they considered it shameful for a woman to let down her hair in public.

Simon was disgusted with the whole thing. He said to himself, "If this man were a prophet, he would know who is touching him and what kind of woman she is–that she is a sinner." His thoughts reek with self-righteousness and faulty assumptions: "If Jesus is really from God . . . and he's probably not . . . he'd know what kind of woman this is . . . and he probably doesn't . . . and he would have nothing to do with her."

The fact is, Simon badly misdiagnosed the problem. Jesus knew exactly what kind of person the woman was. The real problem? Simon didn't know what kind of Savior Jesus was! And Simon didn't realize what kind of sinner he himself was!

What Does Jesus See in You?

To illustrate his point, Jesus told Simon a story about two men who had their financial debts canceled by a gracious moneylender. One man's debt was very large; the other's debt was quite small.

"Which of them will love him more?" asked Jesus.

"I suppose the one who had the bigger debt canceled," Simon replied.

Turning to the woman, Jesus asked Simon, "Do you see this woman?"

Interesting question. Of course Simon saw her with his eyes, but he didn't really see the woman. Simon saw a problem; Jesus saw a person. Simon saw a nuisance; Jesus saw a need. Simon saw a situation to avoid; Jesus saw a chance to help.

Jesus saw more love in that streetwise woman than he saw in the do-everything-by-the-book Pharisee. Standoffish and cautious, Simon hadn't offered Jesus even the basic social courtesies: a kiss of greeting, water to wash his feet, a bit of oil for his head. Awkward but sincere, the woman had washed and kissed Jesus' feet and anointed him with perfume. Her sin-debt was great, but so was her love when the debt was canceled. Jesus saw her sin, but he also saw her potential. He forgave her, and she went away that day in peace (Luke 7:48-50).

How Do You See Your Sin?

When Jesus looks at you, he understands you just as well as he understood the woman at the Pharisee's dinner party. He sees your needs and hurts, your problems and frustrations, your strengths and weaknesses. And face it: he sees your sin.

Sin means breaking God's law (1 John 5:17). It's doing what we shouldn't do and neglecting what we should do (James 4:17). Sin means "trespassing" or stepping over the boundary lines God has established. It means thinking wrong thoughts as well as doing wrong actions (Matthew 5:21-28). It leads to a destructive pattern of self-deception and spiritual imprisonment from which only Jesus can set us free (John 8:31-36; James 1:14, 15).

It's quite unsettling to picture ourselves standing for judgment before a perfect God. "All have sinned and fall short of the glory of God," the Bible says, and "the wages of sin is death" (Romans 3:2; 6:23). Yet the Bible also tells us about God's solution for sin and death. We can be "saved by grace" (Ephesians 2:8-10). This means salvation is a free gift, something we could never earn or deserve because of our own good works. "The gift of God is eternal life in Christ Jesus our Lord" (Romans 6:23). Jesus Christ paid the penalty for our sins and took upon himself the punishment we deserve (Isaiah 53:5, 6; Romans 5:6-8; 1 Peter 2:24).

"God's kindness," the Bible says, "leads you toward repentance" (Romans 2:4). In response to God's mercy, it's only natural to feel deep sorrow or remorse for our sin. Repentance also means being willing to change—to turn from sin and a self-directed life to obeying God in a Christ-directed life.

At Simon's dinner party, Jesus told his Pharisee host that the woman who wet his feet with her tears had many sins—but they had been forgiven "for she loved much."

Have you breathed the sweet aroma of Jesus' love? Does his love move you to live for him?

"Repent, then, and turn to God, so that your sins may be wiped out, that times of refreshing may come from the Lord" (Acts 3:19).

REFLECTIONS

For discussion with a Christian friend:

1. Eventually many of the Jewish leaders themselves became followers of Christ (Acts 6:7). Do you think it was hard for them to swallow their pride and change their minds about Jesus?

2. Sadly, Christians sometimes reflect Simon's critical attitude. It's wrong when Christians avoid people and associate only with "folks like us." God's desire is to grow a church where "there is no Greek or Jew, circumcised or uncircumcised, barbarian, Scythian, slave or free, but Christ is all, and is in all" (Colossians 3:11). Does this kind of church sound appealing to you? Why? Do the churchgoers you know remind you more of Jesus, or of Simon the Pharisee?

3. Do you realize that you have sinned against God? Are you willing to let him be the Lord (ruler) of your life, and bring every part of your life under his loving authority?

For further reading:

Luke 13:5; 24:45-47
Acts 2:38

A DOER AND A DOUBTER: TOUCHING AND TELLING THE TRUTH

Two of the most famous characters in the Bible are Peter, a rough-cut fisherman who became a great "fisher of men," and Thomas, known for his doubt. Yet on closer examination, these two men serve as positive examples of the bold faith Jesus wants from all his disciples.

Going Public

Simon Peter was an eyewitness of Jesus' life and teachings. He was privileged to live up-close with the Lord on a daily basis. Peter was amazed when Jesus invaded his professional world by telling him exactly where and how to catch enormous numbers of fish (Luke 5:1-11; John 21:1-14). He was there when Jesus walked on water, and ventured out onto the water himself until fear overtook him and he began to sink (Matthew 14:22-33). Peter was there at the Last Supper when Jesus washed his disciples' feet, and felt so unworthy that he tried to persuade the Lord not to perform this act of humble service (John 13:1-9).

If you ever struggle to live consistently with your convictions, you can identify with Peter. On the night before Jesus was crucified, Peter boasted that he would never fall away from Jesus even if everyone else did; yet just a few hours later, he denied three times that he ever knew the Lord (Matthew 26:33-35, 69-75). Later though, empowered by the Holy Spirit and sure of Jesus' resurrection, Peter boldly proclaimed his faith even in the face of imprisonment and death (Acts 4:1-22).

It might surprise you to learn that several times in the Gospels, Jesus instructed his disciples not to tell anyone that he was the Christ. Sometimes large crowds gathered simply because they wanted to see the Lord perform miracles, or because they hoped he would lead a rebellion against the Roman government that ruled first-century Israel. Some of Jesus' zealous countrymen even "intended to come and make him king by force," but Jesus "withdrew again into the hills by himself" (John 6:15). He wasn't interested in drawing a crowd; he was determined to fulfill his mission. The crowds were thick but their understanding was shallow, so at that time it was better for people not to spread the word about him.

One time some people brought a man to him who was deaf and who could hardly talk. They begged Jesus to touch the man and heal him. Jesus took the man aside, away from the crowd, then he put his fingers into the man's ears, spit and touched the man's tongue. Looking up to Heaven, Jesus heaved a deep sigh and said, "Be opened!" Immediately, the man was able to hear and speak plainly. Naturally, all those who saw this remarkable miracle wanted to spread the word about Jesus. However, the Bible says, "Jesus commanded them not to tell anyone. But the more he did so, the more they kept talking about it" (Mark 7:36).

The Good Confession

Finally Jesus took some of his disciples aside for a time of private instruction. There he asked them, "Who do people say I am?" His disciples responded, "Some say John the Baptist"–a prophet popular among the common people whose message of repentance sounded similar to the one Jesus was proclaiming. "Others say Elijah"–for the people knew about a messianic prophecy that said God would send Elijah the prophet before the "great and dreadful day of the Lord comes" (Malachi 4:5). According to Jesus, John the Baptist fulfilled that prophecy (Matthew 11:11-14). Still others said Jesus was "Jeremiah or one of the prophets"–for clearly, he was speaking words that came from God.

Jesus pressed his disciples further. "But what about you? Who do you say I am?"

Peter answered, "You are the Christ, the Son of the living God" (Matthew 16:13-16; Mark 8:27-29). Christians often refer to these words as the Good Confession. Peter was confessing (agreeing with, affirming as truth) several important facts:

1. Jesus is the Christ; he is the promised Messiah, God's anointed one.

2. Jesus is the Son of God; he is more than an ordinary man, not merely a great teacher or moral example; he is divine. Later, the apostle Paul wrote that "in Christ all the fullness of the Deity lives in

bodily form" (Colossians 2:9).

3. God is "the living God"–the Almighty One, alive and powerful.

Peter's assessment of Jesus was correct, so Jesus complimented his answer. The fact that Jesus is the Christ is the bedrock truth upon which Jesus promised to build his church (Matthew 16:18). Surprisingly, though, Jesus immediately "warned his disciples not to tell anyone that he was the Christ" (Matthew 16:20). The time still wasn't right.

And besides, even his own disciples still didn't understand what it meant for him to be the Christ. So Jesus began to teach them what it meant: "the Son of Man must suffer many things and be rejected by the elders, chief priests and teachers of the law." He "must be killed and after three days rise again." When Jesus spoke plainly about these things, Peter took him aside and began to scold him. After all, Peter didn't want his beloved Lord to suffer! But Jesus rebuked Peter firmly and told him, "You do not have in mind the things of God, but the things of men" (Mark 8:31-33).

Not Ashamed

Eventually Jesus' command changed from "Don't tell anyone" to "Go tell everyone."

• Jesus said, "Whoever acknowledges me before men, I will also acknowledge him before my Father in heaven. But whoever disowns me before men, I will disown him before my Father in heaven" (Matthew 10:32, 33).

• Jesus said, "If anyone is ashamed of me and my words in this adulterous and sinful generation, the Son of Man will be ashamed of him when he comes in his Father's glory with the holy angels" (Mark 8:38).

• Jesus said, "But you will receive power when the Holy Spirit comes on you; and you will be my witnesses in Jerusalem, and in all Judea and Samaria, and to the ends of the earth" (Acts 1:8).

Remember Thomas–the one we often label "doubting Thomas"? The fact is, he was more courageous and more trusting than we sometimes think. Late in Jesus' ministry, when the Lord boldly headed back to the vicinity of Jerusalem, his disciples knew that going there meant great danger (for Jesus had so many enemies in Jerusalem). But Thomas said, "Let us also go, that we may die with him" (John 11:16).

At the Last Supper, Thomas asked Jesus, "Lord, we don't know where you are going, so how can we know the way?" His clear question resulted in a famous answer from Jesus' lips: "I am the way and the truth and the life. No one comes to the Father except through me" (John 14:5, 6).

Thomas demanded firsthand evidence of Jesus' resurrection before he would believe. In Thomas' defense, he wasn't with the other disciples the first time Jesus appeared to them after the Lord rose from the dead (John 20:24). Plus, the other disciples reacted with doubt as well when they first heard reports that Jesus was alive (Luke 24:9-11). Needing to be sure about something as important as the resurrection, Thomas declared, "Unless I see the nail marks in his hands and put my finger where the nails were, and put my hand into his side, I will not believe it" (John 20:25).

Jesus met the challenge. A week later he stood next to Thomas and said, "Put your finger here; see my hands. Reach out your hand and put it into my side. Stop doubting and believe." And Thomas responded with one of the shortest but most profound confessions of faith in all of Scripture. Firmly convinced, with doubts erased, he reverently said to Jesus, "My Lord and my God!" (John 20:27, 28).

Up-close with Jesus, Peter and Thomas embraced the truth. Then they devoted their lives to telling the truth, proclaiming Jesus as Lord to believers and unbelievers alike. As Peter put it, "We cannot help speaking about what we have seen and heard" (Acts 4:20).

What about you? Are you willing to state publicly and without shame that you believe in Christ? Someday, God declares, "at the name of Jesus every knee should bow . . . and every tongue confess that Jesus Christ is Lord, to the glory of God the Father" (Philippians 2:11).

Eventually we're all going to acknowledge that Jesus is Lord. Why not begin now?

REFLECTIONS

For discussion with a Christian friend:

1. The fact that Peter saw Jesus up-close and personal for approximately three years makes it even more impressive when he later wrote that Jesus "committed no sin, and no deceit was found in his mouth" (1 Peter 2:22). If Jesus had ever said or done anything wrong, Peter would have been in a position to know it, yet he affirmed Jesus' sinlessness. Why would such a perfect Lord associate with an imperfect disciple like Peter?

2. Which of Jesus' disciples do you identify with more–Peter, or Thomas? Why?

3. Are you willing to go public with your faith in Jesus? Are you willing to tell others that you believe in the Lord–even when you're with people who don't believe?

For further reading:

Matthew 16:16-23
1 Timothy 6:11-16
1 Peter 3:15

AN AFRICAN OFFICIAL: TASTING THE GOODNESS OF GOD

While visiting my missionary friends in Ethiopia, Dan and Sue Burton, I saw fascinating wildlife. A wildcat sped across the road in front of our truck as we bumped along a country road. We spied baboons in the hills nearby. Monkeys chattered outside the window of the room where I slept. Dan and Sue's young sons played with a tortoise that lived in their yard.

In the capital city of Addis Ababa, I awoke in the morning to the sounds of a loud Arabic cry–the Muslim call to prayer. Dan took me to visit a leprosy hospital where people–many of them missing body parts due to that terrible disease–were weaving cloth to sell. One young girl, perhaps 15 years old, had no hands but she was weaving a beautiful tablecloth with her feet. I thought, If she can do that with no hands, what am I doing with the two hands I have?

Blessed Are the Poor in Spirit

My favorite part of visiting Ethiopia was seeing the Christians there. Most of them were quite poor, but their joy was obvious. In simple church buildings with dirt floors and plain wooden benches, they sang and listened intently while preachers explained God's Word. One man showed me his well-worn Bible. He'd hidden it for 17 years, he said, while the Communists governed the land, for they would have confiscated it and imprisoned him for being a Christian. In a grass hut, a slender, dignified old patriarch prayed reverently for our meal before we broke bread together–bread made from hand-ground grain and baked on an open fire. During the meal we joked and listened to stories about life in the village. How could there be so much joy amid so much poverty? These people had tasted the goodness of God!

One evening, with the help of an interpreter, I taught a Bible lesson to about 40 people crammed into a tin-roofed house lit by one tiny light bulb. A deaf girl sat in the front row, unable to hear but determined to participate anyway. Nearby sat a young mother nursing her baby, and young men wearing gobis, long flowing cloths the Ethiopians wrap around them at night. This must be a lot what it was like in Jesus' day, I thought, as I looked around at the crowd. I thought about the time Jesus "looked at those seated in a circle around him and said, 'Here are my mother and my brothers! Whoever does God's will is my brother and sister and mother'" (Mark 3:34, 35).

Jesus came to earth to reconcile lost people—to bring us back to God and restore the peaceful relationship we lost because of sin. He came so that we could be members of his family, children of God, born anew into God's household. The apostle John wrote that "to all who received him, to those who believed in his name, he gave the right to become children of God—children born not of natural descent, nor of human decision or a husband's will, but born of God" (John 1:12, 13). Later John's excitement bubbled over as he exclaimed, "How great is the love the Father has lavished on us, that we should be called children of God! And that is what we are!" (1 John 3:1).

According to Jesus, the greatest spiritual blessings

come to those who humble themselves and seek God's kingdom most of all. "Blessed are the poor in spirit," Jesus said, "for theirs is the kingdom of heaven" (Matthew 5:3).

The Bible says, "Taste and see that the Lord is good; blessed is the man who takes refuge in him" (Psalm 34:8). When we humbly embrace the truth of God, among other blessings we experience a deep and abiding sense of peace and joy. It's a peace that transcends all understanding, even when we face all kinds of trouble (John 16:33; Philippians 4:7). It's a joy that strengthens us during life's harshest trials, for we know that the Lord's presence is real, his power great, and his promises true (Philippians 4:4-6; James 1:2-4; 1 Peter 1:3-9).

The Good News About Jesus

Acts 8 tells the true story of a man who tasted God's goodness and discovered the joy of the Lord.

• He was from Ethiopia. This may not correspond exactly to today's geographical boundaries, however, for in those days "Ethiopia" was used in a broader sense to describe the upper Nile region.

• He was an important official who supervised the entire national treasury for Candace, queen of the Ethiopians.

• He was a eunuch, for it was common in some ancient lands to emasculate any men who worked closely with the females in the royal palace.

• He was a worshiper of God who had traveled all the way from northern Africa up to Jerusalem so he could worship the God of Israel.

• He was curious about the Bible. As he traveled back toward Ethiopia, he was sitting in a chariot reading from the Old Testament–Isaiah 53. He was hungry to know the Lord, like the people Jesus talked about when he said, "Blessed are those who hunger and thirst for righteousness, for they will be filled" (Matthew 5:6).

When a Christian named Philip approached the chariot, he heard the man reading aloud from Isaiah and asked, "Do you understand what you are reading?" The Ethiopian answered, "How can I unless someone explains it to me?" Maybe you can sympathize with the Ethiopian. Sometimes it's helpful to have a friend come alongside us and help us understand God's Word. Soon Philip joined the Ethiopian in the chariot and they studied the Bible together as they rode along.

The Ethiopian had another question: "Tell me, please, who is the prophet talking about, himself or someone else?" The verses he had in mind (Isaiah 53:7, 8) refer to someone who was "led like a sheep to the slaughter." Philip began with that Scripture and told the Ethiopian the good news about Jesus. No doubt Philip went on to explain how Jesus fulfilled the messianic prophecies of Isaiah 53 and many others, and how Jesus died on the cross for our sins and rose from the dead.

Why Shouldn't I Be Baptized?

The Bible says, "As they traveled along the road, they came to some water and the eunuch said, 'Look, here is water. Why shouldn't I be baptized?'" Evidently Philip had mentioned baptism while he was talking about the good news of Christ. For the Ethiopian, baptism was a joyous privilege—a natural response for someone who had now come to believe in Christ. He didn't resist it; he requested it.

Baptism, you see, is a beautiful part of our faith-response to God. Before returning to Heaven, the risen Christ told his disciples, "Therefore go and make disciples of all nations, baptizing them in the name of the Father and of the Son and of the Holy Spirit" (Matthew 28:19). The early Christians complied with the Lord's command.

When Peter preached in Jerusalem, "those who accepted his message were baptized" (Acts 2:41). When the people in Samaria "believed Philip as he preached the good news of the kingdom of God and the name of Jesus Christ, they were baptized, both men and women" (Acts 8:12). When the apostle Paul became a Christian, a believer named Ananias encouraged him, "And now what are you waiting for? Get up, be baptized and wash your sins away, calling on his name" (Acts 22:16).

In Greece, new believers like Lydia and her household, the Philippian jailer and his family, and people in the city of Corinth were baptized immediately upon coming to faith in Christ (Acts 16:15; 31-34; 18:8). The result? Joy! The jailer and his family, for example, were "filled with joy, because they had come to believe in God" (Acts 16:34).

Perhaps this raises some questions for you. What about infant baptism? Certainly Jesus loves little children; but there's no example of an infant baptism in the New Testament. People were urged to repent of their personal sin and come to their own faith in Christ prior to being baptized. Aren't we saved by grace? Yes! This wonderful truth is made clear in Ephesians 2:8-10 and other Scriptures. Baptism doesn't deny that we are saved by God's grace; in baptism we affirm and embrace this wonderful truth. The book of Romans explains that we are saved not by our own good works, but by the gracious work of God; yet this same book speaks about obedience of faith (Romans 1:5; 16:26), and says that Christians are "baptized into Christ Jesus" (Romans 6:3). The book of Galatians talks about the futility of trying to earn our own salvation, yet it also mentions that believers are "baptized into Christ." Baptism leads to joy, as repentant believers surrender their lives to Christ.

That's what the Ethiopian discovered. After ordering the chariot to stop, he and Philip went down into the water and Philip baptized him. Baptism was by immersion, a full burial in the water, which is fitting since Christians are "buried with him in baptism and raised with him through your faith in the power of God, who raised him from the dead" (Colossians 2:12). When Philip and the Ethiopian came up out of the water, the Spirit of the Lord led Philip to go elsewhere to preach, but the Ethiopian "went on his way rejoicing" (Acts 8:39).

And so will you, my friend. So will you.

REFLECTIONS

For discussion with a Christian friend:

1. If Christ promises to give us joy and peace, does this mean the Christian life will be easy and trouble-free?

2. Have you been baptized in the way described in the New Testament? If not, why not?

3. According to 1 Corinthians 15:1-4, the death, burial, and resurrection of Christ are the basis of our Christian faith. What does this say about the importance of believing in Jesus? What does it say about the importance of baptism?

4. According to Acts 2:38, who should be baptized? What is the purpose of baptism?

For further reading:

Acts 2:36-41
Romans 6:1-4
1 Corinthians 12:13
Galatians 3:26-29
Ephesians 4:1-6
1 Peter 2:2, 3; 3:21

HUMBLE MERCHANTS: SENSING GOD'S PRESENCE

God wants us to be near him, living in his presence. That wonderful truth is one of the main themes of the Bible.

King David wrote, "Where can I go from your Spirit? Where can I flee from your presence? . . . If I settle on the far side of the sea, even there your hand will guide me, your right hand will hold me fast" (Psalm 139:7, 9, 10).

Because of Jesus' death and resurrection, we can "approach [God's] throne of grace with confidence, so that we may receive mercy and find grace to help us in our time of need." We can "draw near to God with a sincere heart in full assurance of faith" (Hebrews 4:16; 10:22).

The closing pages of the Bible picture the glorious future of God's people. "Now the dwelling of God is with men, and he will live with them. They will be his people, and God himself will be with them and be their God. He will wipe away every tear from their eyes. There will be no more death or mourning or crying or pain, for the old order of things has passed away" (Revelation 21:3, 4).

Sounds wonderful, doesn't it?

When you become a follower of Christ, you embrace these promises and claim them as your own. God has always been over and around you, but now, by your welcoming invitation, he takes up residence in you through his Holy Spirit. You become part of a grand, growing family of believers composed of men and women from all over the world who love and serve the Lord.

Enlarging the Tent

About 2,000 years before Christ was born, God told his servant Abram (later known as Abraham), "I will make you into a great nation and I will bless you . . . and you will be a blessing . . . and all peoples on earth will be blessed through you" (Genesis 12:1, 3). For Abraham, following God meant packing up his family and moving to a new land, living in tents as he looked "forward to the city with foundations, whose architect and builder is God" (Hebrews 11:8-10).

Then about 700 years before Jesus was born, the prophet Isaiah used the imagery of a tent to encourage God's people to enlarge their vision for the future. In those days, tents were made of leather or coarse cloth, fastened down with ropes and wooden pegs. So the prophet said, "Enlarge the place of your tent, stretch your tent curtains wide, do not hold back; lengthen your cords, strengthen your stakes" (Isaiah 54:2). Like an expanding tent, the Lord's kingdom was meant to grow–to take in more and more people who follow the Lord.

A first-century woman named Priscilla and her husband Aquila surely discussed Isaiah's prophecy at length while they cut, measured, and sewed tents in their tentmaking shop. This Christian couple made tents for a living, but their main concern was expanding the family of God. Priscilla and Aquila illustrate what it's like to follow Christ after we take the step of faith and become Christians.

They used their daily work to further God's kingdom work. Priscilla and Aquila made tents alongside the apostle Paul, who was a tentmaker himself. They supported themselves by making tents, but their higher goal was spreading the word of God. Each week on the Sabbath day, Paul (presumably with Priscilla and Aquila accompanying him) went to the Jewish synagogue and tried to persuade people to believe in Christ (Acts 18:1-3).

Once you become a Christian, Jesus is Lord of every part of your life. "Whatever you do," the Bible says, "work at it with all your heart, as working for the Lord, not for men" (Colossians 3:23). "Make it your ambition to lead a quiet life, to mind your own business and to work with your hands," Paul wrote, "so that your daily life may win the respect of outsiders" (1 Thessalonians 4:12).

They shared their knowledge with other disciples. When Priscilla and Aquila heard a brilliant speaker named Apollos teach about the Bible, they realized he was not fully informed. He "spoke with great fervor and taught about Jesus accurately," but "he knew only the baptism of John." In other words, he hadn't heard the full message about the salvation Christ died to bring. Evidently he was uninformed about

Christian baptism and the gift of the Holy Spirit. So Priscilla and Aquila "invited him to their home and explained to him the way of God more adequately" (Acts 18:26). Is there someone you could tell about Jesus? Do you have family members or friends you could help to know the way of God more adequately? How could you humbly share with them what you have learned about the Lord?

They dared to live by extravagant faith. The apostle Paul expressed his gratitude to his friends Priscilla and Aquila, for "they risked their lives for me," he says (Romans 16:4). Faith in Christ might not make you literally risk your life, but it will certainly move you to lay down your life in other ways–through sacrificial service, generous giving, and willing obedience to the Lord's will.

They opened their home to God's people. The church met at Priscilla and Aquila's house (Romans 16:5; 1 Corinthians 16:19). In those days there were no church buildings like we have today, but people like Priscilla and Aquila realized how important it was for Christians to gather together, so they exercised hospitality and opened their home to the believers.

How could you use your home to serve the Lord? Whatever the meeting place, do you realize how important it is to gather together regularly with other Christians? When the family of God gets together, you will hear the Bible taught, you'll partake of the Lord's Supper in remembrance of Jesus, you'll learn to pray and give and serve and love. And you'll do all this alongside others who, like you, have learned to sense the presence of God. That's why the Bible says, "Let us not give up meeting together, as some are in the habit of doing, but let us encourage one another" (Hebrews 10:25).

Continuing the Journey

Jesus told his followers to "go and make disciples of all nations." A disciple is a follower, an apprentice, a student of the Master, and discipleship is an ongoing journey. As disciples of Jesus, we have a lot to learn. That's why the Lord said we should continue teaching new disciples to obey everything he has commanded (Matthew 28:19, 20).

Obedience to Christ is the logical response to his loving lordship. Jesus said, "If you love me, you will obey what I command" (John 14:15). He asked, "Why do you call me 'Lord, Lord,' and do not do what I say?" (Luke 6:46). His commandments are not a burden (1 John 5:3), for he always has our best interests at heart. But Jesus was honest about the demands of discipleship.

In one sense, it costs you nothing to become a Christian. Salvation is the free, unmerited gift of God (Romans 6:23). But in another sense, it costs you everything to become a Christian—for Jesus expects us to yield every part of our lives to his authority (Luke 9:23; 14:33).

When you become a Christian, it isn't the end of the journey. It's only the beginning. Accepting Christ isn't a graduation; it's a birth. It isn't the finish line; it's the starting gun of a marathon race. It isn't an announcement to the world that you've got it all together and you're now completely mature. It's the beginning of long process of spiritual growth, with the Lord as your partner. It's not just a casual commitment or a one-day-a-week obligation; it's a lifestyle. You have become a lifelong follower of Christ!

No doubt Jesus realized how daunting all this would sound, so he made a wonderful promise to us: "I will be with you always, to the very end of the age" (Matthew 28:20).

If the Christian life looks like a big challenge, remember: You aren't in this alone! The Lord promises to be with you always, in every place and every situation, on every step of your spiritual journey.

That's what happens when you embrace the truth.

THE HOLY SPIRIT

Scripture calls the Holy Spirit our Comforter or Counselor (John 16:7), the Spirit of truth (John 16:13), the Spirit of holiness (Romans 1:4), the Spirit of God or Christ (Romans 8:9), and the Spirit of grace (Hebrews 10:29). Scripture also uses several word pictures to show us what the Holy Spirit is like: a dove (Matthew 3:16), living water (John 7:37-39), and a "seal" or deposit of our future inheritance (Ephesians 1:13, 14). God's Spirit lives in us when we belong to Christ. Our bodies are his temple (Acts 2:38; Romans 8:14-16; 1 Corinthians 6:19). He helps us bear the wonderful fruit of Christlike character, "the fruit of the Spirit" (Galatians 5:22-26). He gives us gifts or abilities we can use to serve in the church, the body of Christ (Romans 12:4-8; 1 Peter 4:10, 11). He helps us pray, especially during times of intense suffering (Romans 8:26, 27). He gives us inner strength (Ephesians 3:16; Philippians 4:13).

REFLECTIONS

For discussion with a Christian friend:

1. Could you use some extra strength from God? Christians receive extra strength to live as God desires, through the power of the Holy Spirit. What signs of God's presence do you see in the lives of Christians you know? What signs of God's presence do you see in your own life?

2. Read Galatians 5:22-26. What do you think it means to say the sinful part of yourself has been "crucified"?

3. First Thessalonians 5:19 says, "Do not put out the Spirit's fire." Is there anything in your life that is throwing cold water on the Spirit's work right now? How can you fan the flame?

For further reading:

Acts 2:42-47
Ephesians 4:1-32